Dips and Spreads

Gia Scott

Copyright © 2014 Gia Scott

All rights reserved.

ISBN: 1495407004
ISBN-13: 978-1495407000

DEDICATION

For my mom, who has always been the queen of the kitchen.

Table of Contents

DEDICATION iii

ACKNOWLEDGMENTS i

Introduction 1

Cold Dip Recipes..3

Almost Hummus Dip 3

Bean Dip 4

Braunschweiger Dip...4

Chicken Liver & Onion Dip..5

Cold Crab Dip 6

Cooked Salsa 7

Corned Beef Dip..8

Cottage Cheese Dip..8

Crab Rangoon Dip...9

Curry Dip 10

Easy Chipotle Cheese Dip..10

Easy Mediterranean Shrimp Dip 11

Fat Free Ranch Dip 11

Ford Motor Company Dip 12

Guacamole..12

Harlequin Dip 13

Red Bean Dip 14

Hot Dip Recipes 15

Broccoli & Mushroom Dip 15

Burger Dip 16

Hot Cheese Dip 16

Hot Wing Dip 17

Parmesan Artichoke Dip 17

Pepperoni Pizza Dip 18

Spinach Artichoke Cheese Dip 19

Spinach Oyster Dip 20

Seven Layer Taco Dip 21

Southern Bean Dip 22

Vegetable Dip 23

Spreads 24

Bacon Cheese Ball 24

Bologna Sandwich Spread 24

Chicken Almond Spread 25

Chipotle Cheese Spread 26

Ham & Cheese Log 27

Mexican Cheese Spread 28

Smoked Salmon Spread 29

Three Cheese Ball 30

Bonus Chapter-Crackers & More! 31

Bagel Crisps 31

Butter Crackers 32

Cheese Wafers	33
Homemade Melba Toast	34
Modern Pilot Crackers	35
Rye Crackers	36
Saltine or Soda Crackers	37
Wheat Crackers	38
Creative Presentation	40
Ladies Brunch or Night Out	40
Break Up Hand Holder	41
Guy's Night or the Man Cave's Delight	41
Movie Night with the Family	41
Dressing to Impress	42
Tailgating with the Crowd	42
The Picnic	43
ABOUT THE AUTHOR	44
Links	46

ACKNOWLEDGMENTS

I want to thank my mom, my husband, my children and grandchildren for always believing in me.
Without that belief and their help, I wouldn't be half the person I am.

Introduction

Dips and Spreads is a collection of thirty seven different dip and spread recipes, plus an entire **bonus chapter** of *Crackers and More!* With such variety, everyone is sure to find a favorite, whether old or new. The bonus chapter will let you make your own crackers, with a variety of options from Homemade melba toast to traditional saltine or soda crackers.

Whether for chips or veggies, hot or cold, dips are part of the array of foods used for both appetizers and snacks. Some are quick and simple, while others are more elaborate and complicated to make. They are great for picnics, movie nights, casual get-togethers with friends, cocktail parties, tailgating, ballgame munchies, and almost any occasion. I hope you find a new favorite among the offerings here.

This book presents you with a variety of choices, flavors, preparation methods, and presentation choices to suit a wide variety of circumstances, regions of the country, and personal tastes. From fresh seafood as an ingredient to pantry staples, there is plenty of variety to be found.

Never forget the basic rule of recipes: they are nothing more than a guideline. Adjust seasonings to your tastes, but start with a small amount. You can always add more, but it is very difficult to take some back out!

Cold Dip Recipes

Almost Hummus Dip

3 cans garbanzo beans, drained & rinsed
1 jar roasted red pepper, drained & coarsely chopped
¼ c. extra virgin olive oil
4 cloves garlic, peeled & minced
1/3 c. lemon juice
1 can pitted black olives, drained
1 ¼ tsp. salt
½ tsp. ground black pepper
½ tsp. curry powder
½ tsp. ground coriander
½ tsp. ground cumin
½ tsp. oregano, crushed
1 tsp. lemon zest
1 small can chopped black olives

Put everything except the chopped black olives into a blender and puree until fairly smooth. Scrap ingredients into bowl, stir in chopped black olives. Refrigerate several hours or overnight tightly covered. Serve with crackers, flatbread, or pita chips.

Bean Dip

1 can refried beans
1 tbsp. lime juice
½ minced jalapeno
1 tbsp. olive oil
1 tbsp. water
½ tsp. salt

Combine ingredients in bowl, mixing well with fork. Heat in microwave in 1 minute intervals, stirring after each cycle, until hot. Serve with corn or tortilla chips.

Braunschweiger Dip

8 oz. braunschweiger
2 c. plain yogurt
1 tsp. Worcestershire sauce
1 tbsp. onion powder
1 tsp. salt
½ tsp. pepper
2 tbsp. dried minced onion

Put all ingredients into a blender and blend until evenly combined. Refrigerate 1 hour or overnight to blend flavors. Serve with crackers or melba toast.

Chicken Liver & Onion Dip

¼ c. water
½ c. finely chopped onion
1 tbsp. salt
1 tsp. onion powder
1 tsp. garlic powder
¼ tsp. black pepper
½ tsp. beef bouillon granules
1 boiled egg, peeled & finely chopped
¼ c. mayonnaise
1 tsp. Worcestershire sauce
¼ tsp. liquid smoke flavor
1 tbsp. cooked crumbled bacon

Place chicken livers in small saucepan and add water to cover. Simmer over medium heat 8-10 minutes or until tender. Drain and set aside.

Place all ingredients except boiled egg and bacon into blender. Blend for 30-60 seconds or until smooth. Stir in half of bacon and chopped egg, reserving remainder for garnishing dip. Refrigerate until serving.

Cold Crab Dip

1 c. crabmeat
8 oz. blue cheese, room temperature
8 oz. cream cheese, room temperature
1 tbsp. lemon juice
2 tbsp. mayonnaise
½ tbsp. Worcestershire sauce
½ c. thinly sliced water chestnuts

Combine cheeses. Add remaining ingredients and mix well. Serve with crackers, raw vegetables, or chips.

Cooked Salsa

This is a simple cooked salsa. Like other salsas, it is best to store them in non-metallic containers because of the acids present in the foods. While it can be served hot or warm, the cold temperature with the "heat" from the chili peppers provides a pleasant contrast that enhances the flavors. Try them with a salad too!

2 cans chopped tomatoes (or 2 cups of peeled, chopped tomatoes + ½ c. tomato juice)
1 onion, finely chopped
1 clove garlic, finely minced
2 tbsp. cider vinegar
1 tsp. oregano
1 tsp. cumin seeds
4 poblano peppers, roasted, peeled, & seeded
2 Anaheim peppers, roasted, peeled & seeded
1 jalapeno pepper, roasted, peeled & seeded
1 tsp. chili powder
1 beef bouillon cube
1 can black beans, drained & rinsed
1 can whole kernel corn, drained

Chop peppers coarsely. Combine all ingredients in medium saucepan. Heat salsa mixture over medium heat until it just begins to boil, stirring occasionally. Reduce heat to simmer, simmer about 30 minutes. Remove from heat, and put into glass or plastic containers with tight sealing lids. Refrigerate until served. Salsa keeps for up to a week in the refrigerator.

Corned Beef Dip

1 (12 oz.) can corned beef
1 envelope onion soup mix
2 c. sour cream or Greek yogurt

Combine all ingredients. Cover and chill for at least 1 hour before serving. Keep refrigerated until served.

Cottage Cheese Dip

1 ½ c. cottage cheese
2 tbsp. lemon juice
4 tbsp. buttermilk
2-3 green onions, sliced with tops
1 tsp. onion powder
1 tsp. garlic powder
1 tsp. black pepper

Blend cottage cheese, lemon juice, and buttermilk until smooth. Add remaining ingredients and blend again. Serve with vegetable dippers.

Crab Rangoon Dip

2 c. crab meat
16 oz. cream cheese, softened
½ c. sour cream
4 green onions, chopped
1 ½ tsp. Worcestershire sauce
2 tbsp. powdered sugar
½ tsp. garlic powder
½ tsp. lemon juice

Combine softened cream cheese and chopped green onions. Stir in crab meat, sour cream, Worcestershire sauce, powdered sugar, garlic powder, and lemon juice. Place in small baking dish and bake for 30 minutes or until hot & bubbly at 350 degrees F.

Serve hot with chips or fried wontons.

Curry Dip

1 tsp. minced garlic
2 c. mayonnaise
5 tbsp. ketchup
Dash of Tabasco
1 ½ tsp. Worcestershire sauce
2 tbsp. curry powder
½ tsp. salt

Combine all ingredients. Cover and refrigerate at least one hour before serving.

Serve with vegetable dippers such as celery, carrots, cucumbers, radishes, etc.

Easy Chipotle Cheese Dip

16 oz. plain yogurt
8 oz. shredded sharp cheddar cheese
4 oz. shredded Swiss cheese
½ tsp. salt
1 tsp. (more or less to taste) Tabasco chipotle pepper sauce

Combine all ingredients in bowl and beat with mixer until blended. Refrigerate until serving.

Easy Mediterranean Shrimp Dip

16 oz. plain Greek yogurt
1 c. finely chopped cooked shrimp
2 tbsp. lemon juice
1 pkg. zesty Italian dressing mix

Combine yogurt, lemon juice and dressing mix. Stir until evenly combined. Gently stir in shrimp. Cover and refrigerate for at least one hour. Best if refrigerated overnight before serving.

Fat Free Ranch Dip
Great with everything from veggies to French Fries!

16 oz. fat free yogurt
3 tbsp. garlic powder
1 tbsp. garlic salt
1 tsp. black pepper
1 tsp. salt
3 tbsp. onion powder
2 tbsp. parsley flakes
1 tbsp. dill weed

Combine all ingredients, stirring to evenly distribute the seasonings through the yogurt. Cover tightly and store in refrigerator at least 4 hours and preferably overnight before serving.

Ford Motor Company Dip

I have no idea why it refers to Ford, but I can only assume that at one point, the recipe was included with some publication put out by Ford. It's an old recipe, but it has a simplicity that is timeless.

3 pkgs. (8 oz.) cream cheese, softened
2 c. mayonnaise
6 tbsp. minced onion
4 tbsp. horseradish sauce
Generous dash of Tabasco sauce
Pinch of salt
Tsp. chopped parsley or parsley flakes

Beat cream cheese until fluffy. Add remaining ingredients and beat to a smooth consistency. Chill until serving.
Serve with crackers or potato chips.

Guacamole

2 ripe avocados
2 tbsp. sour cream
1 tsp. lemon or lime juice
1 tbsp. finely minced onion
1 tbsp. finely minced jalapeno pepper

Peel & seed avocados. Mash with fork and add lemon juice, continuing to mash and blend lemon juice with avocado pulp. Add remaining ingredients and combine with fork. Best served promptly with tortilla chips.

Harlequin Dip

2 tbsp. milk
12 oz. cottage cheese
1 tsp. lemon juice
½ tsp. salt
1 tsp. horseradish sauce
1 medium carrot, sliced into 1 inch pieces
3 radishes, halved
3 sprigs fresh parsley

Put milk, cottage cheese, lemon juice, salt and horseradish in blender. Cover and run on high speed until mixture is smooth. Add remaining ingredients and blend on low speed just until vegetables are chopped. Chill dip before serving.

Red Bean Dip

1 (15 oz.) can kidney beans, rinsed & drained
1 small onion, finely chopped
1 small green bell pepper, seeded and finely chopped
4 slices bacon
dash of garlic powder
dash of salt
dash of black pepper
4 slices bacon
1 c. sour cream

Mash kidney beans and set aside. Fry bacon until crisp. Remove bacon from pan and set aside. Sauté onion and bell pepper until onion is soft and translucent in bacon drippings. Add mashed kidney beans and mix thoroughly. Stir in seasonings and sour cream. Crumble bacon and add to mixture.

Put mixture into container and cover. Refrigerate one hour or overnight before serving.

Hot Dip Recipes

Broccoli & Mushroom Dip

1 onion, finely chopped
8 oz. mushrooms, chopped
1 tbsp. finely minced garlic
½ c. butter or margarine
1 16 oz. pkg. frozen chopped broccoli
1 10.75 oz. can cream of mushroom soup
8 oz. cream cheese

Cook broccoli according to package directions. Drain.

In skillet over medium heat, melt butter. Add onion and sauté until limp and translucent. Add garlic and mushrooms. Sauté for 4-5 minutes. Add broccoli, canned soup, and cream cheese. Stir until cheese is melted.

Pour mixture into chafing dish or mini-slow cooker to keep warm while serving. Serve with melba toast, sturdy crackers or chips.

Burger Dip

1 lb. hamburger
1 can chopped tomatoes
1 can tomatoes with chilies (such as Ro-Tel)
3 bunches green onion, chopped
¾ c. diced roasted red pepper
½ tsp. oregano
½ tsp. ground cumin
1 tbsp. minced garlic
1 sm. can tomato paste
1 tbsp. chili powder
8 oz. grated sharp cheddar cheese

Brown hamburger, onions, and garlic. Add remaining ingredients except cheese. Cook over low heat for about 45 minutes to blend flavors. Stir in cheese and serve hot with corn chips or tortilla chips.

Hot Cheese Dip

This is also very good drizzled onto tacos, tostadas, and enchiladas.

1 c. cubed cheese spread (like Velveeta)
1 can diced tomatoes with green chilies & onions
½ jalapeno, minced

In small saucepan, heat tomatoes and jalapenos until boiling over medium heat, stirring occasionally. Add cheese, and stir constantly until melted. Serve with tortilla chips.

Hot Wing Dip

1 (8 oz.) pkg. cream cheese
2 c. finely chopped cooked chicken
½ c. hot wing sauce (use your favorite)
¼ c. crumbled blue cheese
1 green onions, sliced

Spread cream cheese in the bottom of a microwavable 9" pie plate.

In a small bowl, combine chicken and hot wing sauce. Pour mixture over cream cheese and spread evenly. Sprinkle with blue cheese.

Microwave mixture on high for 2 minutes or until thoroughly heated. Sprinkle green onions over top and serve with celery sticks as dippers.

Parmesan Artichoke Dip

1 (14 oz.) can artichoke hearts, drained and chopped
1 c. mayonnaise
1 c. grated Parmesan cheese
1 tbsp. minced garlic

Heat oven to 350 degrees F.
Mix all ingredients until evenly combined. Spread in a 9" pie pan. Bake mixture 20-25 minutes or until golden brown and bubbly.

Pepperoni Pizza Dip

1 (8 oz.) pkg. cream cheese
1 tsp. Italian seasoning
1 c. (4 oz.) shredded mozzarella cheese
¾ c. grated Parmesan cheese
1 (8 oz.) can pizza or spaghetti sauce
4 oz. sliced pepperoni, coarsely chopped
2 tbsp. chopped green pepper
2 tbsp. thinly sliced green onions

Beat cream cheese and Italian seasoning until fluffy. Spread in a 9" microwave safe pie plate.

Combine mozzarella and Parmesan cheeses. Sprinkle half of cheese over the cream cheese. Top with half of the pepperoni, pizza sauce, cheese mixture, green pepper and onion. Sprinkle remaining pepperoni over the top and microwave uncovered for 2-3 minutes or until cheese is melted, rotating a half turn several times. Remove from microwave and let stand for 2-3 minutes before serving. Serve with breadsticks or crackers.

Spinach Artichoke Cheese Dip

10 oz. box frozen chopped spinach, thawed & drained
14 oz. can artichoke hearts, drained & chopped
1 c. grated Parmesan-Romano cheese blend
½ c. shredded mozzarella cheese
1 c. prepared alfredo sauce
1 tbsp. minced garlic
4 oz. cream cheese, softened

Preheat oven to 350 degrees F.

Combine cream cheese, alfredo sauce, and garlic in bowl, using mixer to blend. Add cheeses. Stir in spinach and artichokes.

Scrape mixture into small baking dish. Bake for 30 minutes or until mixture is bubbling and melted.

Spinach Oyster Dip

4 (10 oz.) pkgs. frozen chopped spinach
4 tbsp. butter
2 tbsp. flour
2 tbsp. chopped onion
$\frac{1}{2}$ c evaporated milk
$\frac{1}{2}$ c. spinach liquor
1 tsp. Worcestershire sauce
$\frac{1}{2}$ tsp. pepper
$\frac{3}{4}$ tsp. celery salt
$\frac{3}{4}$ tsp. garlic salt
6 oz. pepper jack cheese, cut into cubes
Tabasco sauce or other pepper sauce to taste
2 pints fresh oysters, drained and quartered

Cook spinach according to package directions. Drain and reserve $\frac{1}{2}$ c. liquor.

In large skillet, melt butter and add flour. Cook and stir just until blended and smooth; do not brown. Add onion and cook until soft. Add liquids and whisk continuously to prevent lumping. Cook until mixture is smooth and thick.
Add seasonings and cubed cheese. Stir until cheese has melted and then add spinach. Gently add oysters to spinach mixture and cook, stirring often, for 5 minutes. Keep warm while serving in chafing dish or small slow cooker.

Serve with toasted bread or crackers, and will serve 25 guests generously.

Seven Layer Taco Dip

16 oz. refried beans
1 pkg. taco seasoning
16 oz. sour cream
1 c. guacamole
1 c. salsa
1 c. lettuce
1 c. shredded Mexican blend or mild cheddar cheese
1 (4 oz.) can sliced olives
1 c. chopped fresh tomato
1 c. sliced green onions

Spread beans in a layer on serving platter.

In a small bowl, combine sour cream and taco seasoning. Stir mixture until evenly mixed, and then spread over the beans in an even layer. Chill layers for about 1 hour to firm sour cream.

Spread guacamole over sour cream mixture, then top with salsa. Put shredded lettuce over salsa, then sprinkle with cheese. Scatter tomatoes evenly over surface. Sprinkle olive slices over tomatoes. Chill until serving time.

Southern Bean Dip

2 tbsp. tomato juice
2 tbsp. vinegar
3 ½ c. (2 regular cans) pork & beans
dash of cayenne
½ c. cubed processed American cheese (like Velveeta)
1 tsp. garlic salt
1 tsp. chili powder
½ tsp. salt
4 slices bacon, fried crisp

Put all ingredients except bacon into blender. Cover and puree until smooth. Pour into microwavable casserole dish and heat until bubbly, stirring occasionally to ensure even heating.

Crumble bacon to garnish before serving. Serve with chips or crackers.

Vegetable Dip

1 c. mayonnaise
1 c. sour cream
1 tbsp. parsley flakes
1 tsp. dill weed
1 tsp. seasoned salt
1 tbsp. onion powder

Mix all ingredients together and chill for at least one hour. Serve with vegetables.

Spreads

Bacon Cheese Ball

8 oz. sharp cheddar cheese, shredded
8 oz. cream cheese, room temperature
¼ lb. butter (not margarine), room temperature
½ c. crumbled cooked bacon
¼ c. coarsely chopped cooked crisp bacon

Put butter in mixing bowl. Beat until fluffy with electric mixer. Add cream cheese and beat again. Stir in shredded cheese and ½ c. bacon. Shape into a ball, roll in coarsely chopped bacon, and wrap tightly and refrigerate until firm, at least one hour. May be made two days in advance.

Serve with crackers or cocktail bread slices.

Bologna Sandwich Spread

8 oz. bologna
8 oz. shredded American cheese
8 oz. cream cheese, softened
½ c. mayonnaise
½ c. dill pickles, drained and chopped
¼ c. minced onion

Using food processor, coarsely chop bologna.

In mixing bowl, beat cream cheese until smooth. Beat in mayonnaise, pickles, and onion until evenly combined. Stir in cheese and bologna.

Serve with crackers.

Chicken Almond Spread

4 oz. cream cheese
½ tsp. celery salt
½ tsp. onion salt
1 tsp. Worcestershire sauce
dash of Tabasco sauce
1/3 c. sour cream
¼ c. toasted almonds, finely chopped
½ c. cooked chicken
½ c. mushrooms, sliced
1 tsp. olive oil

Sauté mushrooms in olive oil over medium heat for 5-6 minutes. Set aside to cool.

Mix softened cream cheese with celery salt, onion salt, Worcestershire sauce, Tabasco sauce, and sour cream. Stir in almonds, chicken, and mushrooms. Place in serving dish. Garnish with parsley. Refrigerate at least 4 hours (preferably overnight). Serve with melba toast or crackers.

Chipotle Cheese Spread

This is hot stuff, so if you don't like it spicy, you may want to spread it extra thin or cut the amount of peppers in half. It is also a great addition for tacos.

3 chipotle peppers in adobo sauce (more or less to taste)
½ c. plain yogurt
8 oz. cream cheese
1 c. shredded mozzarella cheese
¼ c. julienned sun dried tomatoes in olive oil
½ tsp. salt

In blender, combine chipotle peppers and yogurt. Puree until smooth. Beat cream cheese until smooth. Beat in pepper mixture and salt. Add mozzarella cheese and tomatoes, beating again for 1 minute on medium high speed. Chill until time to serve.

Serve with crackers or bread.

Ham & Cheese Log

4 oz. extra sharp cheddar cheese, shredded
1 (8 oz.) pkg. cream cheese, softened
1 (4 ½ oz.) can deviled ham
½ c. pitted chopped ripe olives
½ c. finely chopped pecans

In small mixing bowl, beat cream cheese until smooth. Stir in cheddar cheese. Add deviled ham and olives and stir until evenly combined. Shape into a log and then roll in chopped pecans, coating evenly. Wrap tightly and chill for at least one hour before serving.

Mexican Cheese Spread

1 (8 oz.) pkg. cream cheese, softened
½ c. plain Greek yogurt
1 (4 oz.) can chopped green chilies, drained
½ tsp. ground cumin
1 tsp. dried oregano, crumbled finely
1 tsp. salt
½ tsp. cracked red pepper
1 roasted poblano pepper, peeled & chopped
1 plum tomato, chopped finely
2 c. shredded Monterey Jack cheese
1 c. shredded sharp cheddar cheese

In mixing bowl, beat cream cheese and yogurt together until smooth and creamy. Stir in green chilies, cumin, oregano, salt, red pepper, poblano pepper, and tomato just until evenly combined. Add cheeses and stir until evenly mixed. Tightly pack mixture into serving container, cover, and refrigerate at least four hours to blend flavors.

Smoked Salmon Spread

2 (8 oz.) pkgs. cream cheese, softened
12 oz. smoked salmon, finely chopped
3 dashes Worcestershire sauce
3 drops Tabasco Chipotle pepper sauce
1 tsp. chopped fresh dill weed
2 tbsp. chopped green onion

In mixing bowl, beat cream cheese until smooth. Stir in remaining ingredients and mix well. Can be served immediately or refrigerated until 1 hour before serving. Best flavor is when mixture is at room temperature.

Serve with plain crackers to let the salmon flavor to be the star.

Three Cheese Ball

1 (8 oz.) pkg. cream cheese, softened
2 c. shredded cheddar cheese
8 oz. blue cheese, crumbled
1 c. pecans, finely chopped
½ c. fresh parsley
¼ c. green onion, minced
1 tsp. Worcestershire sauce
¼ tsp. garlic powder
¼ tsp. onion powder
¼ c. toasted sesame seeds

In a mixing bowl, combine the three cheeses. Stir until evenly mixed. Add nuts, parsley, onion, Worcestershire sauce, garlic powder, and onion powder. Stir to combine.

Shape mixture into a ball. Wrap tightly in plastic wrap and chill at least one hour. Before serving, remove from refrigerator and roll in toasted sesame seeds.

Serve with crackers.

Bonus Chapter-Crackers & More!

This chapter is your bonus chapter, featuring recipes for crackers and other delightful ways to dip and spread.

Bagel Crisps

2 bagels, sliced vertically into $\frac{1}{8}$" slices
Butter flavored spray

Spread bagel slices onto a baking sheet that has been lightly sprayed with butter flavored cooking spray. Spray bagel slices with spray lightly. Turn all slices over, and spray again. Bake in preheated oven for 15 minutes. Turn bagel slices over and bake 15-30 minutes or until dry and crisp. Cool completely before storing up to 3 days in a tightly sealed container.

After bagel slices have been sprayed with butter flavored spray, they may be sprinkled with onion or garlic powder for flavor variations.

Use bagel crisps as dippers with a variety of dips.

Butter Crackers

2 c. flour
3 tsp. baking powder
1 tbsp. sugar
½ c. dehydrated butter powder (mail order item)
½ tsp. + another 1 tsp. salt for topping
6 tbsp. cold butter
2 tbsp. vegetable oil
$2/3$ cup water

Preheat oven to 400 degrees F.

Combine flour, baking powder, butter powder, and ½ tsp. salt in bowl. Cut in butter until mixture resembles fine crumbs. Stir in vegetable oil until a slightly larger crumb forms. Using a mixer on low, gradually add the water, a few tablespoons at a time, until a soft dough forms. Stop mixer, and divide dough in half.

With one half, roll out as thin as possible. Cut into desired shape, pressing straight down without twisting. Place cut out crackers on parchment covered cookie sheets. Re-roll scraps and cut out again. When first pan is full of cut out crackers, sprinkle each cracker lightly with salt, pressing grains of salt lightly into cracker. Prick a few times with a sharp, pointed object. Bake in preheated oven for ten minutes or until crackers just begin to brown.

Cheese Wafers

1 ½ c. flour
½ c. margarine
8 oz. sharp cheddar, shredded
½ tsp. red pepper
1 c. finely chopped pecans

Combine all ingredients in mixing bowl. Beat together just until evenly combined. Divide dough into thirds, and shape each third into a log about 1 ½" diameter. Wrap tightly and refrigerate for at least one hour or until firm.

Preheat oven to 450 degrees F.

Slice into ¼" thick slices and bake on a lightly greased baking sheet for 8-10 minutes or just until edges are golden brown.

Homemade Melba Toast

8 slices white bread

Preheat broiler to high. Toast bread on both sides, taking care to not scorch bread.

Cut off crusts, and holding toast flat, peel the two halves apart so that you have two pieces from each piece of bread that were originally toasted.

Cut each piece of toast into four triangles, and then toast under broiler, untoasted side up, just until golden and edges curl.

Best served warm.

To make ahead, prepare melba toast as directed. Just before serving, place in oven preheated to 325 degrees for 5 minutes, uncovered, before serving.

Modern Pilot Crackers

1 ½ c. milk
4 c. flour
4 tbsp. butter or butter flavored shortening
4 tbsp. brown sugar
1 tbsp. salt

Mix flour, sugar and salt. Cut in butter until it seems to "disappear" into the flour. Stir in milk to make firm dough. Roll dough out to about ½" thick and cut into 2-3" squares. Prick each square with a fork or knife several times.

Bake at 400 degrees F turning several times for 20-25 minutes or until golden brown. Let cool completely before storing in an air tight container. Makes about 24 2" crackers.

Rye Crackers

2 c. rye flour
1 tbsp. caraway seed
1 ½ tsp. salt
1/3 c. oil
1 tsp. honey
¼ c. water (or as needed)

Combine rye flour with caraway and salt. Stir in oil and honey. While stirring, slowly add water until mixture forms a ball. Press together firmly, cover and let rest for 10 minutes.

Preheat oven to 375 degrees F.

Divide dough into fourths. Roll out each portion on lightly floured surface as thin as possible. Cut into 1 ½" squares, and then place on baking sheet with about ½" between each cracker. Prick each cracker several times with a fork.

Bake crackers in preheated oven for 10-12 minutes or until edges start to brown. Remove to cooling rack immediately. Cool completely before storing in an airtight container for up to three months.

Variations: These crackers can be varied in much the same way as the Wheat Crackers.

Saltine or Soda Crackers

2 c. flour
1 tsp. salt
½ tsp. baking soda
2 tbsp. butter
2/3 c. milk

Preheat oven to 375 degrees F.

Combine flour, salt and baking soda. Cut in butter until mixture looks like crumbs. Stir in milk. Form mixture into a ball and knead a few times to make it into a smooth ball. Divide dough into thirds.

Taking one portion of dough, roll out very thin on a lightly floured surface. Lay sheets on ungreased cookie sheet. Sprinkle with salt and prick with a fork. Cut into 1 ½" squares with a sharp knife or pizza cutter. Bake in preheated oven for 10-12 minutes or until lightly browned.

Cool on rack. When completely cool, store in airtight container for up to three months.

Wheat Crackers

1 ¾ c. whole wheat flour
1 ½ c. flour
¾ tsp. salt
1/3 c. oil (use your favorite)
1 c. water
sea salt (for sprinkling)

Preheat oven to 350 degrees F.

Mix flours and salt together. Pour in oil and water. Stir just until blended. Divide dough into two even portions.

One half at a time, roll dough as thin as possible. Place entire sheet of dough on ungreased baking sheet, and score dough with knife but do not cut entirely through dough. Sprinkle evenly with salt, and prick each cracker a few times with fork a few times.

Bake for 15-20 minutes in preheated oven until light brown. Cool crackers on rack. When cool, separate into individual crackers.

Variations:

Cracked Pepper Crackers: add ½ tsp. freshly ground pepper to flour mixture and proceed with recipe as directed. When dough is placed on pan, sprinkle with salt and fresh coarsely ground black pepper lightly, then prick with fork. Bake as directed.

Garlic Crackers: Add 1 tbsp. garlic powder to flour mixture before adding oil. Proceed as directed. After placing dough on baking sheet, substitute garlic salt for regular salt before pricking with fork.

Onion Poppy Seed Crackers: Add 1 tbsp. poppy seeds and 2 tbsp. minced dried onion to flour before adding oil and water. Proceed as directed and substitute onion salt for regular salt after dough has been placed on baking sheet.

Italian Parmesan Crackers: Add 1 tbsp. Italian seasoning and $\frac{1}{2}$ c. dried grated Parmesan cheese (the box kind) to flour before adding oil and water. Proceed as directed; using garlic salt in place of regular salt after dough is placed on cookie sheet.

Sesame Seed Crackers: Add $\frac{1}{4}$ c. sesame seeds to flour mixture before adding oil and water. Proceed as directed.

Southwestern Crackers: Add 2 tbsp. chili powder (hot or mild), $\frac{1}{4}$ tsp. oregano, and $\frac{1}{2}$ tsp. whole cumin to flour mixture before adding oil and water. Proceed as directed.

Creole Crackers: Add 2 tbsp. Tony Chachere's More Spice to flour and omit salt. Proceed as directed; substituting more Tony Chachere's More Spice for the salt after dough is placed on cookie sheet. Prick with fork and bake as directed.

Creative Presentation

Be creative in serving your homemade dips and spreads! Skip the everyday plastic ware with the snap on lids and go for something a bit different. You don't have to be a master decorator or famous television personality to achieve something that is fun, attractive, and appealing.

Ladies Brunch or Night Out

Go for elegant or feminine and flowery! Mismatched china, especially soup bowls, plates, and serving platters can often be found at flea markets and antique shops for reasonable prices. Sometimes, our family and friends have an assortment. Don't worry about matching anything—the more patterns, the merrier! Put spreads and dips in soup bowls or serving bowls, or even keep something on ice by filling a serving bowl with crushed ice and nestling the soup or berry bowl inside of the ice.

Go for the flowers! Using inexpensive clear plastic ware from the dollar store, press fresh flowers flat between two containers, filling the inner container with the dip or spread. (Choose small, delicate flowers for best results, such as violets, pansies, etc.) Put matching flowers between two clear plates or platters for crackers, and more blooms can be scattered onto tables and put in vases to carry the theme along. Extra femininity can be delivered with bits of lace and ribbon, whether alongside pressed flowers or on the table top.

Use things in a different way! What's wrong with putting your dips and spreads in containers that are not usually used for presenting food? Try champagne or wine glasses, martini glasses, or even things that are not food containers at all as holders for inexpensive plain clear plastic or glass containers that are actually in contact with the food.

Break Up Hand Holder

Face it, sometimes the break up hits hard, and it's time to hold a friend's hand and try to cheer them up with a night in and a bunch of comedies or old movies. Skip the romantic stuff and avoid the cookies-and-ice-cream binge with plain jane serving. Stick to smaller containers to reduce the urge to over-indulge in food therapy.

Guy's Night or the Man Cave's Delight

Think manly thoughts as you approach this one. No flowers or lace are needed here! Miniature buckets for dips and spreads can be lined with clear plastic containers. Larger buckets can be lined with plastic wrap or even brown paper to hold chips or crackers. Even plain cardboard boxes can become man cave acceptable décor!

Movie Night with the Family

Sometimes it's just plain okay to use those familiar plastic storage containers from fridge to serving without dressing them up. After all, having fun is sometimes more important than figuring out how to do all of those dishes.

Dressing to Impress

Maybe you are having the boss over, or your prospective in-laws, but whoever it is, you want to impress them a little bit. What then?

Bake or buy small round loaves of bread (6-8" diameter) Cut out a circle on the top of the loaf, then pull out the bread (save it for something else or toast it for breadcrumbs for casseroles) to leave a shell about 1" thick. Put your spreads into the bread bowls for serving. These may also be toasted the day before, wrapping them tightly after they have cooled. Fill just before serving.

For dip containers, visit the vegetable aisle. Big, blocky bell peppers that sit squarely on their bottoms are great containers for veggie dips. Cut off their tops and remove the seeds and seed membranes from inside.

In the fall, pumpkins come in a variety of sizes and have a convenient empty space inside once you cut off the top and scoop out those seeds. Just remember, the shells need prepared and it takes a bit of time. They also can be prepared the night before, covered tightly and refrigerated.

Tailgating with the Crowd

Tailgating is a lot of fun, but it can be a bit chaotic as well, especially when friends all get together, dragging along *their* other friends too. This isn't the time to bring your best china, or even your best plastic ware storage containers. Bring along inexpensive ones, and put a piece of tape on the bottom with your name and phone number—you just MIGHT get the container back!

Stick to the basics, after all, you really would prefer to have fun over devoting yourself to grilling sliders and sautéing mushrooms, wouldn't you?

The Picnic

The picnic is really a smaller scale and quieter version of tailgating. It's also not the best time for your good china or plastic ware. In fact, depending on the occasion, it may even be a great time to focus on disposable rather than anything else. It's also important to keep cold foods cold and hot foods hot. That means preventing melting ice from turning your special cheese spread into cheese goop.

Refreezable ice packs are great for preventing the heat from getting to your food while also not getting it soaking wet. Make sure all foods are tightly sealed, and put your ice or ice packs on top to keep the heat at bay. Don't leave your ice chest in the sun, and make sure the lid is latched after it is opened. It's always best to have drinks in a different cooler than the food, as the drink cooler will be accessed far more often than the food.

If your cooler gets warm inside, there is a saying that tells you how to handle it. **If in doubt, just throw it out.** Nobody's special dip or spread (or other food item) is worth risking food poisoning for!

ABOUT THE AUTHOR

Gia Scott was born, just like everyone else, but she also was born to a family that included politicians, used car dealers, and horse traders. Along with that illustrious lineage, she was related to vaudeville performers, horse trainers, cowboys, entrepreneurs, teachers, and preachers. With such diversity surrounding her from childhood, she still managed to grow up and develop a deep love of books. It was only natural that along the way, she would write them too. *The Survivors: The Time of Chaos* is her first published novel. More will undoubtedly follow. *Freak Files: The Unexplained Tales* is a collection of stories believed to be true to life.

After decades of experimental cooking, much to her family's chagrin (after all, the family is inflicted with the less-than-wonderful versions that never see print!) Gia began writing food articles and a food blog. It was inevitable that cookbooks would follow. This is the thirteenth cookbook. Previous titles include: *All Chocolate—Easy & Economical Recipes Anyone Can Make At Home, 55 Fantastic Fudges, The All American Biscuit, 56+ Marvelous Homemade Mixes, 55*

Frightfully Fun Foods, *A Home Style Thanksgiving*, *At Grandma's Stove*, *The Poverty Perspective Cookbook: Recipes for Rock Bottom Budgets* and *My Precious Cookbook*. Most titles are available in both print and digital editions.

Today, after many incarnations along the way, Gia Scott lives in Mississippi with her husband, three dogs, and two cats in a funny little house surrounded by very big and gnarly trees. Having reached that age of privilege, she can often be found in her garden, wearing peculiar clothes and tending her plants. When she can talk her husband into it, they enjoy going for road trips, looking for the elusive town of New Hope. In between road trips and gardening, she manages to fit in an internet radio talk show called **the Dawn of Shades**, interviewing a variety of people, including other authors, and promoting causes dear to her heart.

In addition to all of that, she still maintains blogs on general topics, cooking & food, and camping, emergency preparedness & outdoors activities. She also helps with content for websites.

Links

To email Gia Scott, mailto:giascott@exogenynetwork.com

Gia's other books can be found at http://bit.ly/GiaBooks

Gia's general blog is found at www.giascott.wordpress.com.

Gia's food blog is found at www.gulfcoastfoods.wordpress.com.

Gia's camping blog is found at www.getreadygo.wordpress.com.

Her author page on Facebook is found at www.facebook.com/giascottblogs

Made in the USA
Monee, IL
05 July 2023